# AMBW

## ASIAN MEN BLACK WOMEN MOVEMENT

## LOVE JOURNEY

AMBW: ASIAN MEN BLACK WOMEN MOVEMENT

# AMBW

## ASIAN MEN BLACK WOMEN MOVEMENT

### BY

### LOVE JOURNEY

## COPYRIGHT

# DEDICATED

This book is dedicated to all the brown girls around the world that love Asian men.
Because I know that Asian men love brown girls too.

# #AMBWLOVE

# TABLE OF CONTENTS

# BRIEF SUMMARY

In AMBW: Asian Men Black Women Movement, writer Love Journey talks about interracial relationships between Asian Men and Black Women and the growth of the AMBW community.

In this first book navigating the exciting world of interracial dating - specifically Asian Men and Black Women - Love Journey explores the who, what, where, when, and why of this unique group.

This is more than just a resource guide.

In an effort to promote healthy relationships between AMBW, Love Journey digs deeper into the movement by discussing the pioneering efforts of Asian men and Black women bravely dating outside the traditional box, ignoring double standards, and expanding their dating options.

AMBW: ASIAN MEN BLACK WOMEN MOVEMENT

# IMPORTANT TERMS

**AMBW –**

Asian Men Black Women Couples

**Black -**

In this book, the terms "Black" and "African American" are used interchangeably to refer to American-born persons who are descendants of African ancestors.

**Asian -**

The term "Asian" will be used to refer to people either born in or descendants of a number of Asian countries including but not limited to: Afghanistan, Bhutan, Cambodia, China, India, Indonesia, Japan, Laos, Malaysia, Maldives, Mongolia, Myanmar (Burma), Pakistan, Philippines, Singapore, South Korea, Taiwan, Thailand, Vietnam, and the Pacific Islands.

AMBW: ASIAN MEN BLACK WOMEN MOVEMENT

# INSIDE THIS GUIDE

The growth of the AMBW movement is an exciting and timely topic.

First, contrary to likely first impressions, this book is not about the exclusion of one race for another - far from it. This book is more about inclusion, the acceptance of men and women of other races as dating options. Readers will NOT find ranting or degrading statements about Asian women or Black men here. Just research data.

This book is an exploration of two beautiful groups of people that have stepped outside of traditional expectations and bravely broadened their horizons; they have become open to the possibility of experiencing romantic happiness with each other.

One important goal is to counter some of the arguments that Asian men and Black women might use to dismiss the possibility of finding love with someone of another race. The author provides a sound argument for why

Asian men and Black women should look beyond negative stereotypes and consider a quality partner in each other.

The message: Be open to the possibilities.

The author paints a clear picture that encourages Asian men and Black women to have the courage to reach beyond color barriers, excuses, stereotypes, and fear, and get to know each other without reservation. Times have changed. We live in a global society, and everyone seems to be finding love abundantly, except Asian men and Black women. Research shows that these two groups are the least likely to be chosen on online dating apps, there is a gender ratio disparity, and there are double standards when it comes to expectations for Asian men and Black women in the dating world. These hindrances have left many Asian men and Black women unmarried, alone, and/or unable to find a suitable mate within their own race.

So, should Asian men and Black women wait forever? The answer is emphatically, "No."

The AMBW movement is a growing community that is debunking the myths that people can only find love and happiness within their own race. This is a long overdue discussion that blows the roof off of old and tired belief systems that are not relevant in today's world.

Good men and women exist in all shapes, sizes, colors, nationalities, and ethnicities (as do bad men and women). Asian men and Black women are beautiful, sexy, educated, and deserve sincere love. The author encourages each of us to ask ourselves - are you really open to finding true love? Are you willing to reach beyond the racial divide and into a vast world of possibilities?

So many notions mentally hold Asian men and Black women back from interracial dating. This book encourages readers to explore their belief systems in an analytical way. If after reading this book you decide interracial dating is not for you - no problem. But this author invites you through this book to re-evaluate and rethink this beautiful trend.

AMBW: ASIAN MEN BLACK WOMEN MOVEMENT

# CHAPTER 1: THE MOVEMENT

AMBW Couples are redefining the rules of love.

Welcome to this exciting exploration of the Asian Men Black Women (AMBW) Movement. The AMBW Movement is simply defined as the rapid rise in the number of Asian men and Black women interracial relationships. The goals of the movement are to celebrate, promote, support, advocate, and campaign for AMBW relationships.

The AMBW Community is a nurturing environment that encourages and celebrates interactions between eligible men and women looking for serious relationships and trying to find love.

Asian men and Black women are trailblazers, trendsetters, and pioneers because they look beyond stereotypes to find love in each other. They are no longer willing to accept what society says about them. These are people who have bravely stepped "outside the box" and are shaking off propaganda labels of "least-desirable," "effeminate men," and "domineering women," and taking the time to see other people as they really are, as beautiful, sexy, intelligent, and passionate individuals with much more in common than differences.

Interracial dating and marriage was once a practice that was frowned upon. Today we are celebrating diversity! For many years AMBW relationships have represented the smallest percentage of marriages. They still do, but statistics show that the number of AMBW interracial marriages has grown substantially over the last few decades, and the world is starting to pay attention.

# CHAPTER 2: THE IMPORTANCE OF AMBW INTERRACIAL DATING

Interracial dating (AMBW in particular) has never been about excluding people from one's own race as a dating option but rather the importance of considering people from other races and ethnicities to date, as well.

What happens when the two least-chosen groups get a little help to face their dating fears and embark on their quest to find love? The AMBW Movement. Yes, Asian Men and Black Women may be the least-chosen groups on online dating apps, but this is not the only reason these two groups are coming together in higher numbers.

In the past, these two groups were the least likely to date outside their race. But not any longer. Asian men and Black women are finally moving beyond stereotypes and letting go of stifling traditions that have held them captive while their dating peers blossom into happy relationships with people of other races and ethnicities.

## INTERRACIAL MARRIAGE GROWTH RATE

2018 marks the 51st anniversary of the 1967 U.S. Supreme Court decision, *Loving vs. Virginia*, which ruled against all anti-miscegenation laws, making interracial marriage legal throughout the United States.

The number of interracial marriages has steadily increased ever since. For instance, in 1967, 3% of U.S. newlyweds were married to a person of a different race. Comparably, in 2015, 17% of U.S. newlyweds were married to a person of a different race.

According to the Pew Research Center, 29% of Asians and 18% of Blacks married someone outside their race in 2015.

AMBW: ASIAN MEN BLACK WOMEN MOVEMENT

## INTERRACIAL MARRIAGE GAPS WITHIN ASIAN AND BLACK RACIAL GROUPS

According to a 2017 Pew Research Center study, there are significant interracial marriage gaps within Asian and Black ethnic groups, including gender gaps.

Among Blacks, men are much more likely to marry someone of a different race. In 2015, 24% of Black men outside their race while just 12% of Black women did. For Black women, though, this is a significant increase from 4.6% in 2010.

For Asians the exact opposite is true. Asian women are much more likely to marry someone of a different race. In 2015, 36% of Asian women and 21% of Asian men married outside their race.

Source:

Pew Research Center

"Key facts about race and marriage, 50 years after Loving v. Virginia."

Author: Kristen Bialik

Website: www.pewresearch.org

AMBW: ASIAN MEN BLACK WOMEN MOVEMENT

## AMBW INTERRACIAL MARRIAGE STATISTICS

According to the U.S. Census Bureau, there were 9,000 married AMBW couples in 2010 (0.3% of all new marriages). Also, only 19% of all Asian/Black marriages are between Asian American men and Black women.

Source:

U.S. Census Bureau (2010)

Table FG4. Married Couple Family Groups, by Presence of Own Children In Specific Age Groups, and Age, Earnings, and Race and Hispanic Origin of Both Spouses.

Link:

https://www.census.gov/population/www/socdemo/hh-fam/cps2010.html

AMBW: ASIAN MEN BLACK WOMEN MOVEMENT

# CHAPTER 3: MYTHS DEBUNKED

Asian men and Black women face a common issue - racial bias in online dating.

Online dating apps have unintentionally exposed society's deep-rooted racism; they track data about people's dating preferences, and the statistics are troubling. Asian men and Black women are at a disadvantage when it comes to online dating and are the least-picked on dating sites. It's sad but true.

## BLACK WOMEN

For Black women, dating in the U.S. can be extremely difficult. Not only does the mass media portray black women in a negative way, but pervasive societal racism predisposes many to believe inaccurate representations of their femininity, personal traits, and character. All of which, inaccurately portray Black women as less desirable than other female ethnic groups.

Just because Black women are undervalued in American society doesn't mean Black women are without value.

Let's take a moment to disprove the myths.

**Myth:** Black people in America are lazy and unintelligent.

False.

Black women are one of the most educated groups in the U.S. and are earning more college degrees than ever before. According to the Brookings Institute, there has been a significant increase in rates of four-year college completion among Black Americans, especially among Black women, who consistently make up more than 50-60 percent of the total number of Blacks who receive postsecondary degrees.

**Myth:** Black women are not attracted to Asian men.

False.

There are many Asian men and Black women who find each other attractive; the AMBW movement is proof of the worldwide shift from this untruth. Black women are finding the courage to admit their attraction to Asian men, shake off the old narratives, and seek out love.

**Myth:** All Black women are gold diggers.

False.

This misinformation is a result of the ubiquitous negative images of Black women presented in music videos, movies, and other media. Despite the constant stream of negative information presented to the public, countless Black women have continued to excel academically, professionally, and raise responsible children. Like any other group of people, there are always some who become exactly as they are portrayed, but these few by no means represent the whole. Black women desire love, marriage, family, and loyalty just like everyone else.

**Myth:** Black women only want black men.

False.

Love has no color. Black women (and other women as well) want to be loved, appreciated, financially secure, respected, and valued. Interracial dating and marriage statistics show Black women are becoming increasingly confident about dating men outside their race. Black women have been programmed not to date outside their race for many generations. But times are changing. Our global society is providing more opportunities for women to open their mind to interracial dating and marriage. Like other groups, Black women are examining their traditions, belief systems, and customs and asking - why not?

**Myth:** All Black women are big, loud, and aggressive (code for masculine).

False.

Black women are women. Women are human. Humans come in all shapes, forms, and sizes.

People, including Black women, are all different in personality and temperament. Some women are loud, and some are quiet. Some are tall, and some are petite. And just so you know, not all black women have a big butt. We all are subject to stereotyping of some kind. Be careful not to group an entire race of people into a narrow point of view.

# AMBW: ASIAN MEN BLACK WOMEN MOVEMENT

## ASIAN MEN

For Asian men in the U.S., the dating world has always been riddled with false narratives and physical and cultural stereotypes. When compared to other men on dating websites, Asian men statistically receive the least number of messages and matches from heterosexual women. Historically, Asian men have been underestimated in U.S. society and depicted as less desirable than white men by mainstream media. Propaganda.

But things are changing.

Asian men have started their own positive image campaign that is proving to the world that Asian men are sexy, masculine, and talented. Proof of their success is found in the rise in popularity of K-pop worldwide and in the fact that Asian men have recently had better representation in movies and films.

Let's take a moment to disprove the myths surrounding Asian men.

AMBW: ASIAN MEN BLACK WOMEN MOVEMENT

**Myth:** Asian Men are not attracted to Black Women.

False.

There are Asian men who are open to dating women outside their race, especially Black women. Some Asian men don't open up about their attraction to Black women because they are afraid of rejection. Other Asian men are hesitant to go against their parent's strict traditional values on same-race marriage. However, like Black women, Asian men are examining their traditions, belief systems, and customs and asking and bravely stepping outside the box.

**Myth:** Asian men only date Asian or White women.

Semi-False.

Unfortunately, many Asian men (especially those outside the U.S.) have never personally met a Black person in their entire lives and have only seen glimpses of them in false media depictions. The only images of beautiful women they have been exposed to are the Asian women they see every day and white women on television. But the old mindset of "Asian only" or "White-is-right" is disappearing as more and more people become aware of the world's great, beautiful diversity. For example, when Asian men and Black women travel and get to know each other, propaganda is discredited in the face of meeting real people.

"Asian guys presume that black women aren't interested in them, and black women only see Asian men associating with other Asians or Whites and assume that's the only type of women they are interested in. So remaining open and keeping yourself attune to the subtle interest as you would with someone of your own culture is the only way you will know for sure. It's better to be turned down than it is to not try and possibly miss out on a beautiful relationship or at the worst outcome you made a great new friend who can help you feel more comfortable for the one who Asian man that may be looking for more." (Shiree McCarver, 2017).

**Myth:** All Asian men have small penises.

False.

Who would have thought that anyone would ever have to put this in a book? Unfortunately, it is such a common stereotype that it keeps some women from even considering Asian men as a dating option. Ladies, this is a lie. Penis size varies from man to man. There are men in all races with varying small, medium, and large penis sizes. Race is not the determining factor, and besides, how important is penis size to you? What is more important: penis size or loyalty? Affection? Love?

**Myth:** Asian men are all small, quiet, and unassertive (code for feminine).

False.

"Weak, effeminate, geeky, unsexy — Asian men are subject to a litany of unflattering stereotypes that cater to society's masculine ideals. Given these negative labels, Asian men often feel that they have to take the extra step to prove to potential partners that they are anything but the stereotypical Asian male... This is about as true as "All Black women are strong, loud, rude and manly." There is a media ideology that some racist made up, and the rest of the world decided to buy into it." (Shiree McCarver, 2017)

Regardless of race, men are men. Men come in all shapes and sizes, some are loud, and some are more reserved. Some are bad, and some are good. Each one is an individual with a distinctive personality and character. Please consider that sometimes a person's demeanor is a product of when, where, and how they were raised. In other words, sometimes cultural differences are what makes another person seem strange. Don't judge a book by its cover; get to know someone before you make a judgment. They might turn out to be Mr. Right.

**Myth:** All Asian men want from Black women is sex.

True/False

Of course, this may be true for some, but not for all. Black women have been over-sexualized in the media for a very long time. Unfortunately, some men have bought into that mirage.

# CHAPTER 4: AMBW INTERRACIAL DATING FACTS

## Why Asian Men and Black Women Should Consider Interracial Dating

**Fact:** Asian men and Black women are more likely to date within their race than their male or female counterparts.

It's time for both Asian men and Black women to look beyond skin color and mass media images and broaden their horizons. Interracial relationships are less taboo than in the past, and the world is becoming more and more diverse. There are some important phenomenon to take into consideration when thinking about dating and marriage.

## Lack of Eligible African American Men

News flash! There is a shortage of eligible black men. How many Black women do you know that have never been married? A significant number of Black women that only date black men remain single year after year for a variety of reasons such as:

Black men are disproportionately over-incarcerated. It is no secret that black men are targeted and imprisoned at a higher rate than any other racial group in America. Statistics prove that while Black males make up only 7 percent of the U.S. population, they represent over 50 percent of the prison population. The result - a lower number of eligible black men in the dating pool.

Black women graduate college at a higher rate than black men. As a result, college-educated black women interested in dating Black men with a college degree face significant difficulties in finding Black men with similar education and income and therefore remain single.

Some black men are gay, which further decreases the number of available Black men to Black women.

Reminder: The purpose of this section is not to put Black men down. These are just the facts and a harsh reality that single black women must take into consideration. Yes, there are good eligible Black men out there - just not enough. Why are 70 percent of Black women continuing to remain single? The answer is that unfortunately Black women have historically limited their dating options and suffered the consequences.

For example, if there is one eligible straight unincarcerated black male for every six eligible straight unincarcerated black females in the United States - it is statistically impossible for every black woman that desires to marry a black man to do so.

Black women, let me ask you this: why not INCLUDE other races IN ADDITION TO Black men and significantly increase your chances of finding love? Black women interested in marriage must expand their options.

## More Options

Black women, let's be real and ask ourselves: If Black men date interracially, why can't Black women? Black men are twice as likely to intermarry (at 24 percent of marriages) than Black women, which further decreases the pool of potential Black male partners for Black women.

Similarly, since Asian women date interracially, why can't Asian men? What are we waiting on?

Asian men and Black women are becoming increasingly more confident about dating men and women outside their race. Without a doubt, interracial dating is the key to increasing the dating options for single Asian men Black women, who significantly outnumber eligible counterparts.

## Asia's Gender Imbalance Crisis

Gender Imbalance – More men than women.

China's One Child Policy, and others like it, have resulted in a son preference culture where boys are perceived as more valuable than girls. It is a fact that son preference cultures in many Asian countries have resulted in high rates of female feticide, female infanticide, abandonment, forced abortions and forced sterilizations which have all led to a gender imbalance. As a result, Asian men outnumber eligible Asian women in one of the largest populated areas of the world.

For example, India and China eliminate more unborn female children than the number of girls born in America every year (It's a Girl, 2012). Female Feticide, also known as Sex-Selective Abortion, is the practice of finding out the sex of an unborn child and aborting it if it is a girl – essentially, the practice of terminating a pregnancy based on the predicted sex of the fetus. In 2011, it was reported that in India five million girls are selectively aborted annually. As a result of sex-selective abortions, there is a growing gender gap between the number of men versus women in adulthood, which has impacted the population and growth rates in certain countries.

From 1979 to 2015, China implemented the One Child Policy, a birth control policy, also known as a population planning measure that restricted families from having more than one child. While the goal was population control, it had the unintended consequence of creating a severe gender imbalance - 37 million more men than women.

Source:
*Discriminated to Death (2017)*
*Gender Issues Harming Women Worldwide*
*Written by Shay Spivey, BSW, MSW*

AMBW: ASIAN MEN BLACK WOMEN MOVEMENT

# CHAPTER 5: MEETING YOUR MATCH

It's true!

There are many Asian men and Black women who find each other attractive. And the AMBW movement across the world is proof of the shift away from the restraints of traditional dating practices.

This next section outlines where to meet Asian Men and Black Women open to interracial dating and resources within the AMBW community. Although the number of AMBW couples are growing globally, AMBW couples statistics make up less than 1% of the comparable US statistics.

Best Cities for AMBW Couples

Online AMBW Resources

AMBW Organizations

AMBW in Print

AMBW Films and Movies

## BEST CITIES FOR AMBW COUPLES

AMBW couples live all across the globe. Following is a list of cities that have the highest concentration of recorded AMBW couple data in 2017.

### Top U.S. States

1. New York
2. Florida
3. Hawaii
4. Maryland
5. California

**New York**

#1 - The top U.S. area for AMBW couples is Queens, New York City, New York.

-Asians make up 26% of the population.

-Blacks make up 18% of the population.

-Has the largest number of married AMBW couples in the US.

Other areas in New York with a high concentration of AMBW couples:

#9 - Bronx - New York City, New York

#10 - Brooklyn - New York City, New York

**Florida**

#2 - The second top US area for AMBW couples is Fort Lauderdale, Florida.

Other areas in Florida with a high concentration of AMBW couples:
-West Palm Beach, FL
-Orlando, Florida
-Miami, Florida

Asian Caribbean men make up more than half of the married AMBW couples in each of these cities with Miami at 91% Asian Caribbean men, West Palm Beach at 86%, Fort Lauderdale at 80%, and Orlando at 62%.

**Hawaii**

Pacific Islander and Filipino men make up the bulk of AMBW relationships in Honolulu, Hawaii.

## California

Los Angeles, California has the greatest diversity of married AMBW couples with Filipino, East Indian, Chinese, Pacific Islander, and Japanese men all showing up frequently in LA married AMBW couples.

## Georgia

Atlanta, Georgia at #3 on the overall list, has a growing Asian population now at 7% of the area's population, and ahead of the total US Asian population percentage at 5%. Atlanta sees a relatively high number of married AMBWs with both Asian men from the Caribbean, as well as with Asian men from South Asia – India, Pakistan, and Bangladesh in particular.

In other news – did you know that Caribbean Asian men have the highest rate of AMBW marriages out of any group of Asian men? The next largest Asian male group to marry Black women are American born Asian men. Last but not least are Asian men born and raised in Asian countries. But as Black women travel abroad more and more, love is bound to be on the horizon.

## ONLINE AMBW RESOURCES

The online AMBW community is huge! In the world of modern dating, meeting people online is common. Following are online resources that specifically cater to Asian men and Black women in their pursuit of friendship and love.

AMBW Information Website

AMBW Dating Websites

Online Groups

Meetup Groups

Facebook Pages & Groups

Blogs, Instagram, Tumblr, Youtube Channels

## Resource - Popular AMBW Information Website

### Asian Black Couples (ABC)

Website: www.asianblackcouples.com

Description: Asian Black Couples is the top place for news, facts, and analysis about Blasian couples.

## Resource - Popular AMBW Dating Websites

Following is a list of popular AMBW dating websites. Asian men and Black women are the two most discriminated groups in online dating websites and have even been labeled as "least desirable." AMBW dating websites provide a tailored environment where eligible Asian men and Black women can look for a serious relationship and try to find love.

### Blasian Love Forever

Website: www.blasianloveforever.com

Facebook: www.facebook.com/BlasianLoveForever

Description:

Founded in 2015. Blasian Love Forever™ (BLF) is a unique online dating site that was created to bring Asian men and Black women (AMBW) together to fulfill their undeniable love attraction between each other.

### Blasian Date

Website: www.ambwdate.com

Description:

Interracial Black and Asian Dating.

Cost: Free

# AMBW: ASIAN MEN BLACK WOMEN MOVEMENT

## Resources - Online AMBW Groups

Black Women, Asian Men United

bwamu2.ning.com/

Black Women Asian Men – The Initiation

https://www.facebook.com/groups/35633047454168
3/

You and Me... We Could Make Blasians

www.facebook.com/groups/2208196674/

Description:

This group is created to foster relationships between Asian men and Black women. This will also serve as a forum for all Asian men and Black women to meet, share, and

grow together.

Asian Man and Black Woman, The Evolutions of Euphoria

https://www.facebook.com/groups/evolutioneuphoria/

AMBW

Website:

https://www.facebook.com/groups/299366753427017/

Description:

We aim to break the notable disparity between Asian men and Black women. Building

communication and friendships around the world.

Asian Boys for Black Girls

Website:

https://www.facebook.com/groups/287509244617906/

Description: Dating Facebook page.

## AMBW Meetup Groups

An excellent way to meet Asian men and Black women in your area is to join an AMBW meetup group or start one in your area. Following is a list of popular AMBW meetup groups.

## AMBW MeetUp

Link: www.meetup.com/topics/ambw

Tokyo, Japan

Tokyo Non-Japanese Women/Japanese Men Network

Website: www.meetup.com/Tokyo-Non-Japanese-Women-Japanese-Men

Estimated 2,835 Members

New York, New York

Asian Men and Black Women Connections (NYC)

Website: www.meetup.com/AMBW_NYC

Estimated 1,294 Members

Washington, DC

Black Women & Asian Men in the DMV

Website: www.meetup.com/BWAMDC

Estimated 686 members

Mountain View, California

Black2Asian - SF Bay Area Fun Events and Cultural Exchange!

Website: www.meetup.com/black2asian

Estimated 638 Members

Los Angeles, California

The Perfect Mixture Interracial Dating

Website:

www.meetup.com/ThePerfectMixtureInterracialDating

Estimated 545 Members

Los Angeles, California

Blasian Connections LA

Website: www.meetup.com/Blasian-Connections-LA

Estimated 538 Members

Dallas, Texas

Asian Men and Black Women in DFW

Website: www.meetup.com/AMBW-meet

Estimated 492 Members

Duluth, Georgia

Red Bridge Society Afro-Asian (Duluth, GA)

Website: www.meetup.com/Red-Bridge-Society-Gwinnett

Estimated 260 Members

Redondo Beach, California

SoCal BWAM (Black Women Asian Men, AMBW, Blasian)

Website: https://www.meetup.com/SoCalBwam

Estimated 260 Members

London, United Kingdom

Black & Asian Community (London)

Website: www.meetup.com/SoCalBwam

Estimated 260 Members

Atlanta, Georgia

Atlanta AMBW Meetup

Website: www.meetup.com/Atlanta-AMBW-Meetup

Estimated 104 Members

Jacksonville, Florida

Fl/Ga Blasian Meetup Group

Website: www.meetup.com/Fl-Ga-Blasian-Meetup-Group

Approximately 88 Members

Virginia Beach, Virginia

BWAM (Black Women and Asian Men) 7 Cities

Website: www.meetup.com/BWAM-7-Cities

Approximately 75 Members


Baltimore, Maryland

Asian Men and Black Women (AMBW) Baltimore

Website: www.meetup.com/AMBWBaltimore

Approximately 60 members


Baltimore, Maryland

Asian Men and Black Women Persuasion (AMBWP) – World Wide

Website: http://www.meetup.com/ambwpworldwide

Approximately 800 members


Hyattsville, Maryland

ISO AMBW

Website: www.meetup.com/ISO-ambw

Approximately 50 Members

Philadelphia, Pennsylvania

Philly Asian Men / Black Woman Rock (AMBW)!

http://www.meetup.com/phillyAMBWrocks/

Approximately 212 members

## Resource - AMBW Facebook Pages & Groups

The Love Life of an Asian Guy

www.facebook.com/theLLAG

AMBW for Life

www.facebook.com/AMBWforLife/

AMBW Channel

www.facebook.com/asianmenandblackwomen/

Vmarie401

www.facebook.com/Vmarie401/

Lily and James's love story

www.facebook.com/lilypetalsworld/

Black Women Asian Men Connection

www.facebook.com/BWAMConnection/

MazeLee

www.facebook.com/MazeLee-845755648865584/

Love Journey

www.facebook.com/lovejourneybooks

A brown girl's love for the world of Asian dramas, culture, food, and music

Black Women Asian Men (The Initiation)

https://www.facebook.com/groups/356330474541683/

You and Me... We Could Make Blasians

www.facebook.com/groups/2208196674/

Black Women in Japan

https://www.facebook.com/groups/322557231281481/

Asian Man and Black Woman,The Evolutions of Euphoria

https://www.facebook.com/groups/evolutioneuphoria/

Black in Korea

Facebook Group: 1,132 members

https://www.facebook.com/groups/blackinkorea/

Asian Man and Black Woman, The Evolution's of Euphoria Group 2

Facebook Group: 943 members,  Lead Admin: Hadivyah Burgess El

https://www.facebook.com/groups/evolutionofeuphoria2/

AMBW

Facebook Group: 934 members

https://www.facebook.com/groups/299366753427017/

Red Bridge Society (AMBW / BLASIAN) GA)

Facebook Group: 881 members

https://www.facebook.com/groups/redbridgesoceitygwinnett/

Asian Boys for Black Girls

Facebook Group; 641 members

https://www.facebook.com/groups/287509244617906/

xBlack Women Asian Men United Sexy Crazy Heart Breakers & Takers

Facebook Group: 198 members

https://www.facebook.com/groups/213247059787/

Black Women With Korean Partners

Facebook Group: 32 members

https://www.facebook.com/groups/43218450351858 0/

AMBW Channel

https://www.facebook.com/asianmenandblackwomen /

AMBW for Life

https://www.facebook.com/AMBWforLife?_rdr

## Resource - Blogs, Instagram, Tumblr, Youtube Channels

Following is a list of popular AMBW blogs, Instagram, Tumblr, and YouTube channels that have gained popularity from their Youtube videos focused on Asian men and Black women.

ambwdate Instagram

https://www.instagram.com/ambwdate/

AMBW for Life Instagram

https://www.instagram.com/ambwforlife/

asian_black_love

https://www.instagram.com/asian_black_love/

Black Women Asian Men

blackwomenasianmen.tumblr.com/

Breaking Bread With An Asian

breakingbreadwithanasian.blogspot.com/

BWAM is Love

http://bwambw.tumblr.com/

Just Peachy

http://www.justpeachy.co/

The Love Life of an Asian Guy

ranierm.wordpress.com/

MazeLee

Creators: Alena Maze, African American, and Joe Lee, Korean American

https://www.youtube.com/user/livinamaze

My Husband is Asian

shashalaperf.blogspot.com/

Primrose Panglea

Creators: Primrose, Zimbabwean British, and Jaspreet, Indian British

https://www.youtube.com/user/BlissfullyEnchanted7

Sardonic Sista Says

rentec.wordpress.com/

Timothy Delaghetto

Creator: Timothy Delaghetto, Thai American  GF: Chia

Habte, Eritrean (African) and Salvadoran

https://www.youtube.com/user/TimothyDeLaGhetto2

## Chinese and Black

Blasian Quest

https://www.youtube.com/c/blasianquest

Celestereille

celestereille.wordpress.com/

Chocolate Chick In China

chocolatechickinchina.wordpress.com/

From Africa To China

https://fromafricatochina.com/

GanDuan Super

https://www.youtube.com/channel/UC6m_Cx8xaLRDx9c9XFtLOBg

Life Behind the Wall

lifebehindthewall.wordpress.com/

My Husband is Asian

shashalaperf.blogspot.com/

## East Asian and Black

East Indian Guys and Black Girls (The Business Page)

https://www.facebook.com/PatraLoverGirl/

Over Mimosas

http://overmimosas.com/

## Japanese and Black

Novel Metropolis

https://novelmetropolis.wordpress.com/

Osaka Yana

osakayana.tumblr.com/

A Piece of Mine

http://eelasor.com/

RamandaBDaisuki Japan

https://www.youtube.com/channel/UC6FHjH9pBMYE-wNtzin9TLA

Ramandab-Daisuki

ramandab-daisuki.tumblr.com/

S-Morishita Studio – Love! Love! Fighting! Comic

www.s-morishitastudio.com/

Smartalecky1

https://www.youtube.com/user/smartalecky1/

Tara Kamiya

tarakamiya.com/

## Korean and Black

Asian Man and Black Wife Blog

http://ambwblog.tumblr.com/

CharlyCheer

https://www.youtube.com/channel/UC-jeysc9SM81n6fWoCiLxtg

ChoNunMigookSaram

https://www.youtube.com/user/ChoNunMigookSaram

The Fairy Godmother of Itaewon

http://thefairygodmotherofitaewon.tumblr.com/

인종 (Injong) Life

https://injonglife.wordpress.com/

J Hearts J
Youtube Channel: 21,250 subscribers

https://www.youtube.com/user/jynsalive

J Hearts J Tumblr

http://jheartsjofficial.tumblr.com/

Sam and Lily Lee

Youtube Channel: 2,470 subscribers

https://www.youtube.com/channel/UCvxOQ48X5NAr4e-oPOvQPRw

SheSpecialDark

Youtube Channel: 533 subscribers

https://www.youtube.com/user/SheSpecialDark

Swirling in the ROK

Youtube Channel: 17 subscribers

https://www.youtube.com/channel/UCreR65TmrQg8TgF-VO832Zg

This Time Now

nearandfar.wordpress.com/about/

Vmarie401: All About Beauty

https://www.youtube.com/user/Vmarie401

**Lao and Black**

Blasian Sensation

https://www.youtube.com/channel/UCJs9B8a3dwFLH
gtFO9n353g

## Tibetan and Black

KC and Camille

https://www.youtube.com/channel/UCLxq3teunPwpEMrwN9md1lA

AMBW: ASIAN MEN BLACK WOMEN MOVEMENT

## AMBW IN PRINT

Following is a list of AMBW focused non-fiction books, comics, manga, and romance novels.

## AMBW Non-Fiction Books, Comics, and Manga

2007

Book: BIAsian Exchanges

Author: Sam Cacas

Description:

BlAsian Exchanges is the story of a Filipino American writer's recollection of his attraction for Black Women and Black culture. To stoke his storytelling, journalist-turned novelist Earvin Ilokano recruits Black women on the Internet to be his muses, and the ensuing e-mail exchanges produce a seemingly endless discussion on cultural and historical similarities among Asian Americans and African Americans and how each group sees each other.

2012/2014/2018

Comic/Manga: Online Comic: Love! Love! Fighting Volume 1, 2, & 3

Author and Artist: Sharean Morishita

Website: www.s-morishitastudio.com

Description:

A beautiful webcomic, Love! Love! Fighting is about a young woman who currently has no money, no job, and her father won't return her phone calls. Stressed and in sore need of a good break, Oriana finds herself in a difficult position when her bossy little cousins trick her back to their home country of South Korea.

*Also available in paperback

2012 - Present

Comic: Saga

Publisher: Image Comics

Genre: Space Opera Fantasy

Illustrated By: Fiona Staples

Written By: Brian K. Vaughan

AMBW Characters: Alana and Marko

2014-2015

AMBW Media Magazine: Colorless World

Author: Asian men Black Women Persuasion AMBWP)

Website: https://issuu.com/ambwp

Description:

AMBW Colorless World Magazine gives the world a chance to see a different side of Asian Men and Black Women. A side that is NOT clouded by stereotypes about what a person should be like because of their race. Instead, AMBW Colorless World Magazine promotes people to focus on the individual and give those individuals a platform to express themselves.

2014

Manga: Forever Wilde

Author: Bebe

Website: www.facebook.com/MyDearBebe/

Description:

The story of ballerina Monet learning to cope with her feelings for brothers Yuan and Jun and uncovering a mysterious secret between them.

2015

Blasian Children's Book: Amy Hodgepodge Series

Author: Kim Wayans and Kevin Knotts

Description:

After years of being homeschooled, Amy Hodges is excited to start fourth grade at a "real" school. But on Amy's first day, she gets teased not only because she's new, but also because she looks different. Amy is African American, White and Asian. Eventually, Amy meets a group of nice kids and one of them even affectionately gives her the nickname "Amy Hodgepodge" since she's a mix of so many races.

2017
Non-fiction: Blasian Invasion: Racial Mixing in the Celebrity Industrial Complex
Author: Myra S. Washington
Description:
A probe into the social construction of race through the mixed-race identity of Blasians, people of Black and Asian ancestry. Washington regards Blasians as belonging to more than one community, given their multiple histories and experiences.

2018

Daisy: A Filipino African American Flower (A Pocketful of Posies)

Authors: Jacy Genesee

Illustrator: Dagmar P.

Description:

Meet Daisy, a half Filipino half African American girl surrounded by the love of two cultures. This book is sure to bring warmth and pride into the hearts of multicultural children all around our beautiful world. Explore Daisy's world as she blossoms in the collection, A Pocketful of Posies.

**AMBW Romance Novels**

AMBW interracial romance is a fast-growing fiction genre where Asian men and Black women are featured together as the heroes, heroines, and love interests. Asian Men and Black Women want to see themselves in their reading material, and authors are delivering. Most AMBW books fall under the interracial & multicultural romance umbrella, but AMBW themes are popping up in other types of fiction as well, such as paranormal, fantasy, sci-fi, mystery, and women's literature.

If reality is reflected in our books, the AMBW movement is growing rapidly. Romance fiction is a billion dollar industry, and more and more authors and readers are focusing on steamy romance novels diverse with color.

No one knows more about how times have changed than popular interracial romance author Shiree McCarver. Twenty years ago, when she wrote her first AMBW book, there wasn't a market for the new romance category. But inspired by her favorite Asian dramas and a desire to see AMBW romance in print, she wrote *J-Pop Love Song: Musicians in Love* (2008) and pioneered a new multicultural & interracial book genre.

Shiree McCarver first fell in love with Japan and the Japanese people after watching Japanese dramas. She started reading more about Japan, the customs, and learning the language. Soon she was devouring Japanese, Taiwanese, and Korean drama and never looked back.

The absence of Black women in these foreign dramas inspired Shiree McCarver to write her first Asian men and Black women romance novel, *J-Pop Love Song: Musicians in Love,* in 2008. Though there wasn't a market for AMBW interracial romance, she received some commercial success.

She wanted to share her love for Asian men and show Black women a new possibility. And so a new interracial book genre was born.

Love Journey is an up and coming AMBW author and AMBW community advocate that I strongly encourage you to check out.

Today there are hundreds of books featuring Asian men and Black women in multiple fiction and non-fiction genres - romance, paranormal, mystery, sci-fi, fantasy, young adult, and women's literature. It's exciting to watch the rapid growth of this new brand. Readers can find AMBW paperback and ebooks in their local libraries, online retailers, and bookstores.

**Fan Fiction**

In addition to, and older than traditionally published AMBW books, is fanfiction. Fanfiction is typically stories written by fans of and featuring characters from, a particular Asian TV Series, movie, music group, etc.

Three popular AMBW fanfiction websites:

Wattpad

Asianfanfics

Tumblr

## AMBW FILMS AND MOVIES

It's no secret that Asian men and Black women are underrepresented in the movie industry. It's rare to see an Asian man and Black women cast in the lead roles of any film, movie, or play – but they do exist. Following is a list of movies, television shows, and/or online videos that feature an Asian Man and Black woman love interest.

1959

Prinsesa Naranja

Actor: Fernando Poe Jr.

Actress: Elizabeth Ramsey

1960's

Television Show:

"Mirror Mirror" (season 2, episode 10 of the original Star Trek series) Nyota Uhura (Nichelle Nichols) "distracts" the alternate dimension version Hikaru Sulu (George Takei) with some very physical flirtations.

1995

Rumble in the Bronx

Actor: Bill Tung Biu

Actress: Carrie Cain-Sparks

1997

Movie: Cinderella (also known as Rodgers & Hammerstein's Cinderella)

Actress: Brandy Norwood

Actor: Paolo Montalban

1997

Movie: Fakin Da Funk

Actor: Danto Basco

Actress: Tatyana Ali

1999

Movie: Catfish in Black Bean Sauce

Actor: Chi Muoi Lo

Actress: Sanaa Lathan

2000

Movie: Romeo Must Die,

Actor: Jet Li

Actress: Aaliyah


2007

Movie: Akira's Hip Hop Shop

Actor: James Kyson

Actress: Emayatzy Corinealdi


2009

Movie: Ninja Assassin

Actor: Rain

Actress: Naomie Harris


2009

Television Show: Flash Forward

Actor: Demetri Noh (John Cho)

Actress: Zoey Andata (Gabrielle Union)

2010

How to Make Love to a Woman

Actor: James Kyson Lee

Actress: Telisha Shaw


2011

Taken From Me: The Tiffany Rubin Story

Actor: Sean Baek

Actress: Taraji Henson


2011

Politics of Love

Actor: Gerry Bednob

Actress: Loretta Devine


2012

Movie: Joyful Noise

Actor: Francis Jue

Actor: Roy Huang

Actress: Angela Grovey

2012

Always Together: Chinese-Jamaicans In Reggae

Documentary about the impact of the Chinese in Jamaican Reggae.


2013

Documentary: Hafu: The Mixed Race Experience in Japan

Documentary which includes David Yano, a Blasian with a Japanese father and Ghanaian mother


2014

Documentary: Finding Samuel Lowe: From Harlem To China

Documentary about Paula Williams Madison searching for descendants of her Chinese grandfather in China.

2015

Someone Else

Actor: Leonardo Nam

Actress: Michaela Waters


2015

TV mini-series: Tut

Actor: Avan Jogia

Actress: Kylie Bunbury


2015-2018

Television Series:

The Disney Channel's KC Undercover, three-part series titled "Double Crossed."

A Blasian romance between Zane (François Chau) and Kira Cooper (Tammy Townsend)


2015

Video Game: Mortal Kombat X (Video game, comic series, mobile game)

Characters: Jacqui Briggs and Takeda Takahashi

2016

Survivor's Remorse

Actress: Tichina Arnold

Actor: Robert Wu


2017

Colored Hearts (Youtube Short Film)

Actor: Kane Lieu

Actress: Robin Johnson


2018

Movie: I'm Having An Affair With My Wife

Actor: William Jeon

Actress: Stacey Malone

AMBW: ASIAN MEN BLACK WOMEN MOVEMENT

# CHAPTER 6: POTENTIAL CHALLENGES

Interracial dating/marriage has the potential to put a severe strain on family relationships. Couples may feel scrutinized under a magnifying glass. Occasionally, the opposition can even be fierce.

Stereotypes. Discrimination. Racism. These can lead to Shock. Discomfort. Anger. Fear. Hate. Judgment. Ultimatums. Threats. Rejection from strangers, family, and friends.

These are any couple's worst fears. AMBW couples aren't immune to discrimination and often face the same challenges.

Change can come as a shock when people are forced to deal with their personal views on race, gender, and ethnicity. Our parents and grandparents come from a different generation when it may have been unacceptable or unsafe to date outside one's race. Their experiences color their perceptions.

However, we now live in a global society, and the world is more diverse than it used to be. While there are cultural differences, there are similarities too. One person's hang-up should not become your hang-up. Life is too short to bypass an opportunity to find true love. If you have found the person who has set your soul on fire and they happen to be another shade of humanity, think twice before walking away.

Hopefully, when families realize that two people really love and care for each other, they will put their differences to the side and embrace you as a couple.

# CHAPTER 7: OUR VOICES

It's with great pleasure that I present a short collection of voices from the AMBW community. I reached out, and Asian men and Black women responded from around the globe with their views about AMBW love. Following is a small sample of the responses, and do not represent the entire collective:

## Question: What brings Asian Men and Black Women together?

*"Well, honestly I truly think that the AMBW movement is very beautiful. I really think it gives both nationalities a chance to learn more about each other and appreciate the person and their culture."*

*"...recently I met an Asian man couple of months ago, and he so far has been the sweetest most caring most honest most compassionate man I know."*

*"Our challenges were that we had been raised in different yet similar ways. Well, I've never been one to believe in stereotypes, and he proves them all wrong in every way."*

*"For me I see more AMBM relationships blooming today than when I was in high school. I feel... AMBW is making its way to being the new norm."*

*"It's so beautiful to see Asian men and Black women couples happy and healthy. I'm excited for people to know about my relationship. Gone are the days of hiding in shadows because of the fear of being judged about*

*being in love with a person who does not meet other people's standard of normal. Love hard, love strong, be beautiful, be bold, be amazing, be proud, enjoy life to the fullest and have a positive outlook on everything. AMBW relationships are going to keep growing so let's keep it moving forward."*

*"We are all human."*

*"Racism and intelligence: Both of us have to overcome racial stereotypes daily."*

*"Having an open mind."*

*"The differences themselves because opposites attract."*

*"Food, laughter, anime, and cosplay."*

*"Sharing the minority experience."*

*"Our cultures. Asian men and Black women share many moral and values. We are taught to respect our elders and humbleness."*

*"The same things that bring any other interracial couple together: common interested, understanding, and an ability to look past a person's race and see the beauty deep inside."*

**Question: What do you think about the Asian men Black women (AMBW) movement?**

*"I love the aspect of breaking with tradition on both sides and following your heart. Falling inlove should not be defined by the color of your skin or background. Love is love regardless of who the person is. So the AMBW movement is just one of the many interracial relationships to make headway."*

*"I love it... I've gained so many friends."*

*"I think it's a long time coming and I'm happy to be a part of it."*

*"With all the stereotypes, ignorance, and unrealistic expectations surrounding Asian men and Black women, who knew that two very different types of people/cultures could find solace and acceptance with each other. What Asian men and Black women share goes beyond the visual perception others see and "exotic" blasian children. We are a dating subculture that (I feel) will change the world as we know it. This is not just interracial dating. This is a shift in the cultural climate. I hope the world is ready."*

*"I like what I like. I'm an equal opportunity dater and open to dating men of all races - I don't discriminate. AMBW is more about inclusion than exclusion to me. I love the Asian culture and crave the opportunity to learn more."*

## Question: Asian men - Tell us about your attraction to black women.

*"There is something beautiful about that melanin... such natural beauty."*

*"I look for certain traits from women, regardless of race. I like intelligent, strong, independent, loyal, caring women. I look for women who love their family and are open to trying new things."*

*"Black women are beautiful."*

*"When I was in school black girls gravitated toward me. I was always the only Asian wherever I went, and they always told me that we vibed so well because of the respect factor. We also shared similarities in our history and the great racial divide in America."*

## Question: Black women - Tell us about your attraction to Asian men.

*"Asian men are very attractive and sexy to me. Asian men, like all other men, come in all shapes, sizes, intelligence levels, and personality traits. But I can't help myself. When I see Asian men, I am easily distracted."*

*"I just love good men."*

*"I grew up in an all-black neighborhood but attended a very diverse school. I always dated outside my race. I don't have a clue why it's just what I preferred."*

*"Asian men have beautiful eyes."*

*"I saw Bruce Lee in "Enter the Dragon" at like ten or eleven years old, and I developed a huge crush on him. Growing up, every Asian boy I'd see would catch my eye and turn my head. I met and became friends with a few, but was always friend-zoned until college. I became more confident in my seductive skills. I love how Asian men carry themselves in a graceful manner and how respectful they tend to be."*

*"My attraction to Asian men started late in life after my best friend invited me over to watch Takeshi Kaneshiro. I adored him enough that I wanted to see more and this is how I found Japanese dramas. Then I found my second love Kimura Takuya."*

*"I'm waiting for my Asian prince charming."*

*"Trust and believe, many of the stereotypes about Asian men are not true."*

*"In my teenage years, I noticed that the only guys that found me attractive were Asian. And they weren't shy about letting me know. Most of my friends, junior high to high school, were Asian. Even in our adult lives, we are still friends and hang out when we can."*

*"I became attracted to Asian men around the age of 17. In high school, I dated a younger Filipino guy with a deep voice, beautiful eyes, and silky black hair."*

*"In 2011, my best friend introduced me to the Korean drama "Boys Over Flowers" and the Korean pop group, Shinee. I was hooked."*

Thank you to everyone that took the time to respond to my call for opinions. This section is a fluid document, and if anyone wishes to add their response for future publications, please send an email to: lovejourneybooks@yahoo.com

# THE END

I hope you found this worthy of a 5-star review.

Good reviews help me tremendously.

Thank you for reading!

AMBW: ASIAN MEN BLACK WOMEN MOVEMENT

# THANK YOU

I love my readers!

Thank you for reading
***AMBW: Asian Men Black Women Movement.***
Though this book is a brief overview, the topic is timely
and this fascinating group is multiplying every day.

If you know of any organizations, groups, events, etc.
that may have been overlooked please send an email to:
lovejourneybooks@yahoo.com

Please join me on my next journey as we explore the
Asian Men Black Women Movement.

AMBW: ASIAN MEN BLACK WOMEN MOVEMENT

# CONTACT

I would love to hear from you!

Email:

LoveJourneyBooks@yahoo.com

Website:

www.ambwlove.com

Twitter & Instagram:

@lovejourneybook

Facebook:

@LoveJourneyAMBWLOVE

Hashtag:

#AMBWLOVE

AMBW: ASIAN MEN BLACK WOMEN MOVEMENT

# OTHER BOOKS BY LOVE JOURNEY

### KPOP Promise Series

Remember Tonight

This Love With U

But I Love You Tonight

### AMBW Romance

Train My Heart

Live Love Aloha

Beautiful Essence

Janya

I Don't Disappoint

Taste of Jasmine

Stay With Me

Black Kyoto Love

Doctor's Desire

Torn

The Only Many By Her Side

### AMBW Sexy Geek Series

Addictive Behavior

A Chance to Love You

## AMBW Winter Romance Series

Saved By The Chase

Chased Back To You

Loved By The Chase

Chased Back To Love

## AMBW Paranormal

Red Night

Her Wildest Dreams

Fated to Love You

## AMBW Fantasy

Her Unexpected Fate

His Unexpected Love

Their Unexpected Legacy

## AMBW Book Bundles / Collections:

KPOP Promise Series 1-3 (Paperback Only)

Sweet Fantasy: Clean Paranormal Romance Collection

Love Language: KPOP Erotic Romance Collection

AMBW Winter Romance Series 1-3

Shades of AMBW: Asian Men Black Women Short Story Collection

Shades of BWWM: Black Women White Men Short Story Collection

Unexpected Series 1-3

**Libro De La Series Promesa KPOP / Spanish Editions:**

Recuerda Esta Noche 1

Esta Amor Contigo 2

Pero Te Amo Hoy 3

AMBW: ASIAN MEN BLACK WOMEN MOVEMENT

# REFERENCES

Adams, S. (2011). *No eHarmony With Asian Men.* Retrieved from https://www.huffingtonpost.com/sunil-adam/no-eharmony-with-Asian-me_b_872507.html

Asian Black Couples (2018). www.Asianblackcouples.com

Asian Black Couples (2017). *Top Asian and Black Couple Websites For 2017 Second Half.* Retrieved from http://asianblackcouples.com/top-asian-and-black-couple-websites-for-2017-second-half/

The Asian American Man, (2017). www.theasianamericanman.com

Bianlik, K. (2017). *Key facts about race and marriage, 50 years after Loving v. Virginia.* Retrieved from http://www.pewresearch.org/fact-tank/2017/06/12/key-facts-about-race-and-marriage-50-years-after-loving-v-virginia/

Brown, A. (2018). 'Least Desirable'? How Racial Discrimination Plays Out In Online Dating. Retrieved from https://www.npr.org/2018/01/09/575352051/least-desirable-how-racial-discrimination-plays-out-in-online-dating

Budden, R., (2017). *Why Millions of Chinese Men Are Staying Single: The gender gap is a big problem in the Middle Kingdom – and its 'leftover men' are going to great lengths to find a wife.* Retrieved from http://www.bbc.com/capital/story/20170213-why-millions-of-chinese-men-are-staying-single

Color Q World (2008). *Chinese blacks in the Americas: The United States.* Retrieved from http://www.colorq.org/MeltingPot/article.aspx?d=America&x=ChineseBlacks

Francisco, E., (2017). *How Tinder Accidentally Exposed Society's Inherent Racism: The five-year-old dating app shed light on an uncomfortable set of stereotypes.* Retrieved from:

https://www.inverse.com/article/36379-tinder-black-women-asian-men-racism

Jayson, S. (2011). *Interracial marriage: More accepted, still growing.* USA Today. Retrieved from http://usatoday30.usatoday.com/news/health/wellness/marriage/story/2011-11-07/Interracial-marriage-More-accepted-still-growing/51115322/1

Kolawole, E., (2015). *Black women face prejudice every day. I don't need it in online dating, too.* Retrieved from https://www.washingtonpost.com/news/soloish/wp/2015/10/12/black-women-face-prejudice-every-day-i-dont-need-it-in-online-dating-too/?utm_term=.ee44d71d06ab

Langhorne Folan, K. (2010). *Don't Bring Home A White Boy: And Other Notions That Keep Black Women From Dating Out.* Karen Hunter Publishing: New York, NY.
Livingston, G. and Brown, A. (2017). *Intermarriage in the U.S. 50 Years After Loving v. Virginia: One-in-six newlyweds are married to someone of a different race or ethnicity.* Pew Research Center. Retrieved from

http://www.pewsocialtrends.org/2017/05/18/interm arriage-in-the-u-s-50-years-after-loving-v-virginia/

Livingston, G. and Brown, A. (2017). *Intermarriage In The U.S. 50 Years After Loving V. Virginia.* Pew Research Center. Retrieved from http://www.pewsocialtrends.org/2017/05/18/1-trends-and-patterns-in-intermarriage/

Louie, S. (2017). *Dating Asian-American Men: The Unspoken Truth.* Retrieved from https://www.psychologytoday.com/blog/minority-report/201706/dating-asian-american-men

McCarver, S. (2017). www.shireemccarver.net

Net Income, (2017). *Jeremy Lin on the "de-masculinization" of Asian men.* Retrieved from https://www.netsdaily.com/2017/4/23/15399394/jeremy-lin-on-the-de-masculation-of-asian-men

Papamarko, S., (2017). *Why black women and Asian men are at a disadvantage when it comes to online dating:*

*Inherent racism plagues the matchmaking world.* Retrieved from:

https://www.thestar.com/life/2017/03/21/racism-and-matchmaking.html

Price, J. and Palomino, A. (2017). *Black Women Share Their Awful Interracial Dating Stories.* Retrieved from https://www.vice.com/en_us/article/nev4kd/black-women-share-their-awful-interracial-dating-stories

Saulny, S. (2012). *Interracial Marriage Seen Gaining Wide Acceptance.* The New York Times. Retrieved from https://www.nytimes.com/2012/02/16/us/pew-study-americans-more-accepting-of-interracial-marriage.html

Schwartz, Z. (2015). *Inside the 'Asian Men Black Women' Dating Scene.* Retrieved from: https://www.vice.com/en_us/article/wd739w/inside-the-asian-men-black-women-online-dating-scene-456

Soong, K. (2016). *Online dating is harder for Asian men. Here's how some have found success.* Retrieved from https://www.washingtonpost.com/news/soloish/wp/2016/08/08/online-dating-is-harder-for-asian-men-heres-how-some-have-found-success/?utm_term=.d719865e42c7

Spivey, Shay (2017). *Discriminated to Death: Gender Issues Harming Women Worldwide.*

Wang, W. (2015). *Interracial marriage: Who is 'marrying out'?* Pew Research Center. Retrieved from http://www.pewresearch.org/fact-tank/2015/06/12/interracial-marriage-who-is-marrying-out/

Yi, D. (2017). *Asian American men aren't taking s*** anymore.* Retrieved from http://www.verygoodlight.com/2017/01/19/asian-american-men/